It's spring!

Bright flowers push up through melting snow.

Sunny spring

Our spring months are March, April and May.

The sun comes up earlier every morning and sets later every evening.

Days are lighter and warmer.

4

An Appleseed Editions book

Paperback edition 2015

First published in 2014 by Franklin Watts
338 Euston Road, London NW1 3BH

Created by Appleseed Editions Ltd,
Well House, Friars Hill, Guestling,
East Sussex TN35 4ET

Designed by Hel James
Edited by Mary-Jane Wilkins

A CIP record for this book is available from the
British Library

ISBN 978 1 4451 3165 8

Dewey Classification: 508.2

Photo acknowledgements
t = top, b = bottom, l = left, r = right, c = centre
page 1 DenisNata/Shutterstock; 3 iStockphoto/
Thinkstock; 5 majeczka/Shutterstock; 6 Hallgerd/
Shutterstock; 7 Ryan McVay/Thinkstock;
8 Anest/Shutterstock; 9 Smileus/Shutterstock;
10 Vishnevskiy Vasily/Shutterstock; 11t&b
iStockphoto/Thinkstock; 12b clearviewstock/
Shutterstock; 13 t&b iStockphoto/Thinkstock;
14 iStockphoto/Thinkstock; 15 visuelldesign/
Shutterstock; 16t iStockphoto/Thinkstock,
b AlessandroZocc/Shutterstock; 17 Steshkin
Yevgeniy/Shutterstock; 18b iStockphoto/
Thinkstock, c Hemera/Thinkstock; 19 Cynthia
Kidwell/Shutterstock; 20 DenisNata/Shutterstock;
21 Jenny Mie Lau King/Shutterstock; 22 t&b
3 iStockphoto/Thinkstock; 23l iStockphoto/
Thinkstock, b Hemera/Thinkstock, r Dirk Ott/
Shutterstock
Cover iStockphoto/Thinkstock

Printed in China

Franklin Watts is a division of Hachette Children's
Books, an Hachette UK company
www.hachette.co.uk

Contents

Nature comes back to life after winter.

Windy weather

It is often windy in spring. This makes the weather change quickly.

One minute it is bright and breezy…

… the next minute
it is pouring
with rain!

Look for a **rainbow**
when sun shines on rain.

Time to grow

Warm spring sun and rain help new plants sprout from the soil.

Leaf buds on tree branches uncurl and *s p r e a d*.

Masses of white and pink
flowers called blossom
open on fruit trees.

Finding food

In spring, many birds fly back
from winter homes further south.
Animals wake from a long, cosy sleep.

Everyone
is hungry!

At the Indian spring festival of Holi, people throw coloured powder everywhere!

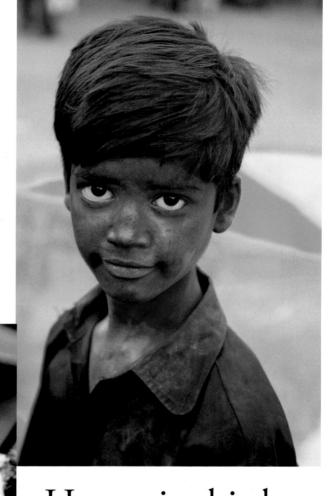

Hummingbirds lay the smallest eggs of all birds. Each egg is the size of a pea.

Useful words

bud
A bump on a branch or stem. Leaves and flowers start as buds.

fawn
A baby deer.

spring
The time of year after winter and before summer.

sprout
To begin to grow above the ground.

Index